# HOW TO USE INSTA 360 X3

A complete guidebook on how to use Insta 360 X3 for beginners

**HOWARD JUSTIN**

# Table of Contents

CHAPTER ONE ..........................................................4

   INTRODUCTION .................................................4

   HOW TO GET STARTED WITH YOUR INSTA360 ...16

   UNBOXING AND INSTALLING YOUR INSTA360 CAMERA .............................................................23

CHAPTER TWO .......................................................31

   BEING AWARE OF THE CAMERA'S FEATURES AND CONTROLS ..........................................................31

   INTRODUCTION TO THE INSTA360 APP AND DESKTOP SOFTWARE...........................................39

CHAPTER THREE.....................................................49

   CAPTURING 360-DEGREE PHOTOS ......................49

   IMMERSIVE 360-DEGREE VIDEOS SHOOTING .....55

   INSTA360 TIME-LAPSE AND HYPERLAPSE ...........63

CHAPTER FOUR ......................................................71

   SHOOTING WITH LONG EXPOSURE AND LOW LIGHT .................................................................71

   A SUMMARY OF THE INSTA360 EDITING WORKFLOW..........................................................79

   PHOTO EDITING WITH THE INSTA360 APP..........86

   VIDEO EDITING WITH THE INSTA360 STUDIO .....92

CHAPTER FIVE ......................................................100

   VIRTUAL TOUR CREATION INTRODUCTION.......100

- STITCHING AND CONNECTING MANY 360-DEGREE PHOTOS ............................................................. 108
- IMPLEMENTING INTERACTIVE ELEMENTS IN VIRTUAL TOURS ................................................. 115
- CONTENT UPLOADING TO SOCIAL MEDIA PLATFORMS ....................................................... 126

CHAPTER SIX ........................................................ 135
- CREATING AND SHARING 360-DEGREE PHOTOSPHERES ON GOOGLE MAPS ................. 135
- COMMON ISSUE WITH INSTA360 AND SOLUTIONS ............................................................................ 142
- STAYING CURRENT WITH NEW FEATURES AND FIRMWARE UPDATES ........................................ 160

CHAPTER SEVEN................................................... 169
- UNBOXING OF THE INSTA 360 X3 ...................... 169
- LIVE STREAMING WITH THE INSTA360 X3 ......... 193
- BEST PRACTICES FOR LIVE STREAMING ............. 198
- THE END ........................................................... 205

# CHAPTER ONE

# INTRODUCTION

360° technology, often known as immersive or spherical media, provides a complete picture of the surroundings from all angles. Unlike standard cameras, which have a limited field of view, 360° cameras use many lenses to capture the full area. This lets viewers access content from any angle, resulting in an immersive experience as if they were physically present in the setting.

**KEY FEATURES OF 360° TECHNOLOGY**

Multi-Lens Setup: Most 360° cameras, like the Insta360 X3, have two or more wide-angle lenses mounted back-to-back. Each lens captures a 180° view, which is then stitched together to form a continuous 360° image or video.

Stitching is the technique of integrating pictures from different lenses into a single, cohesive spherical image. Advanced algorithms ensure that the photos' seams are unnoticeable.

Viewers can navigate 360° content via VR headsets, mobile devices, or desktop interfaces, adjusting their perspective by moving their heads or dragging the view with a mouse or finger.

360° technology has a wide range of applications, including virtual tours, real estate, immersive journalism, gaming, education, and entertainment.

## ADVANTAGES OF USING THE INSTA360 X3

The Insta360 X3 stands out in the market with its extensive capabilities and user-friendly design, making it an excellent choice for both novices and pros in 360° photography and filming.

### Key Benefits of Insta 360 X3

High-Quality Images:

The Insta360 X3 uses high-resolution sensors to capture detailed and vivid 360° images and movies. Advanced image processing offers superb quality, especially in low-light situations.

**Flow State Stabilization:**

This function ensures that the footage remains smooth and stable, even during strong action scenes. Advanced stabilization algorithms remove camera shake, making handheld photography a snap.

**Versatile shooting modes:**

The X3 has several shooting modes, including Standard, HDR, Timelapse, Bullet Time, and more.

These modes enable users to explore and generate unique material.

**User-Friendly Application:**

The Insta360 app offers a simple interface for editing and sharing 360° content. AI-powered editing tools simplify complex operations, allowing users to easily enhance their material.

**Live Streaming:**

The Insta360 X3 offers live streaming, so users can broadcast immersive 360° content in real-time. This tool is very useful for influencers, educators, and event organizers.

**High Build Quality:**

The Insta360 X3 is tough and durable, having been designed to resist a variety of climatic situations. It is water-resistant, making it ideal for outdoor excursions and underwater filming with the right case.

**Portability:**

The X3 is compact and lightweight, making it great for travel, sports, and shooting on the go.

## A BRIEF HISTORY OF INSTA360 CAMERAS

Insta360 was created in 2015 and has quickly become a household name in the 360° camera sector. The company is well-known for its ingenuity and devotion to providing high-quality immersive imaging solutions.

Milestones in the Insta360 Journey:

**2015: Insta360 One:**

The first important release, the Insta360 ONE, revolutionized the market. It included technologies such as FlowState Stabilization and FreeCapture, which enable users to reframe their photos in post-production.

**2016: Insta360 Nano.**

A tiny camera intended for the iPhone that makes 360° photography more accessible to a larger audience. It hooked straight into the phone, allowing for quick sharing and editing.

**2017: Insta360 Pro.**

A professional-grade camera capable of recording 8K 360° video. It was frequently used in virtual reality production and high-end filmmaking.

**2018: Insta360 One X:**

The ONE X made substantial improvements to image quality, stability, and user interface. It gained popularity among action sports aficionados and vloggers.

### 2019: Insta360 GO.

A small, wearable camera that recorded stabilized footage. It was built for everyday usage, with a focus on portability and convenience.

### 2020: Insta360 One R:

A modular camera system that allows users to switch between 360° and regular action camera modules. This adaptability distinguishes it from competitors.

## 2021: Insta360 One X2:

Building on the popularity of the ONE X, the ONE X2 boasted longer battery life, water resistance, and greater stability.

## 2023: Insta360 X3.

The X3 is the latest addition to the range, combining all of the best features of its predecessors with new advances to provide unrivaled performance and user experience in 360° imaging.

Insta360 continues to innovate, pushing the boundaries of what is possible in immersive media, and the Insta360 X3 demonstrates its unwavering dedication to excellence.

## HOW TO GET STARTED WITH YOUR INSTA360

Follow these general steps to get started with your Insta360 camera. Remember that precise instructions may differ depending on the model of your Insta360 camera:

## Charge Your Digital Camera:

Before using your Insta360 camera, make sure it is completely charged. Charge the camera using the included charging cord and power source until the battery is fully charged.

## Insert a MicroSD Memory Card:

Most Insta360 cameras store photographs and videos on MicroSD cards. Insert a suitable MicroSD card into the camera's appropriate slot. Check that the card has enough storage space for your needs.

**Turn On Your Camera:**

By pushing the power button, you can turn on your Insta360 camera. Depending on the model, the location of the power button may differ. Specific instructions can be found in the camera's user handbook.

**Download the Insta360 App:**

On your smartphone or tablet, download and install the official Insta360 app. The app is available for both iOS and Android. This app is required for camera control, file sharing, and access to other functions.

**Connect your camera to the app by doing the following:**

Connect the camera to your smartphone or tablet using the built-in Wi-Fi or Bluetooth capabilities. To establish the connection, follow the instructions in the user handbook. Once connected, you may use the app to control your camera.

**Investigate Camera Modes:**

Learn about the various shooting modes available on your Insta360 camera. Photo, video, time-lapse, and other creative modes may be included. Learn how to use the camera controls or the app to swap between these modes.

**Content Capture:**

Begin taking images and movies by hitting the corresponding camera buttons or using the app controls. Experiment with various settings to get the desired results. Some

Insta360 cameras have novel capabilities such as 360-degree photos and videos.

**Examine and Disseminate:**

After you've captured your content, use the app to go over your images and videos. You can edit, share, and even live-stream your footage to social media networks directly from the app.

**Access Extra Features:**

Investigate any extra features or accessories that came with your Insta360 camera. This could include customized lenses, mounts, or other extras that will expand your creative options.

For extensive instructions and troubleshooting suggestions particular to your model, always refer to the user manual that comes with your Insta360 camera. This will enable a seamless and comfortable exploration of your Insta360 device's possibilities.

# UNBOXING AND INSTALLING YOUR INSTA360 CAMERA

Unboxing and configuring your Insta360 camera is a simple process. Here's a general overview to get you started. Keep in mind that depending on the model of your Insta360 camera, the particular instructions may differ slightly:

**Unboxing:**

Take out the packaging:

Remove any wrapping material before carefully opening the box.

Examine the user manual for all of the components listed.

**Examine the following items:**

Examine the material for a time. The Insta360 camera, charging cable, user handbook, and any additional accessories or mounts are typical components.

**Charge Your Digital Camera:**

Check that your Insta360 camera is fully charged before using it. Connect the camera to a power source and completely charge it using the included charging wire.

## Getting Started:

Insert a MicroSD memory card:

Locate your camera's MicroSD card slot. Insert a MicroSD card with appropriate storage capacity that is compatible with the device. Specific card requirements can be found in the user handbook.

## Turn On Your Camera:

By pushing the power button, you can turn on your Insta360 camera. The location of the power button changes depending on the model, so consult the user manual if necessary.

**Install the Insta360 application:**

On your smartphone or tablet, download and install the Insta360 app. The app is available for both iOS and Android. If you need to create an account, follow the instructions.

**Connecting the Camera to the App:**

Enable the Wi-Fi or Bluetooth capability on the camera. To connect your camera to the

Insta360 app, launch the app and follow the on-screen instructions. This allows you to remotely control the camera and transfer files.

**Firmware update (if required):**

Check the Insta360 app for firmware upgrades. If updates are available, follow the on-screen instructions to update your camera's firmware for improved performance and additional capabilities.

**Investigate Camera Modes:**

Familiarize yourself with your camera's many shooting modes, such as photo, video, time-lapse, and any special modes unique to your model. The camera controls or the app can be used to swap between various modes.

**Content Capture:**

Begin taking images and movies by hitting the corresponding camera buttons or using the app controls. Experiment with different settings to become acquainted with the camera's features.

**Examine and Disseminate:**

Review and manage your captured content with the app. Directly from the app, you may edit, share, or live-stream to social media networks.

**Access Extra Features:**

Investigate any extra features or accessories that come with your Insta360 camera, such as special lenses or mounts. The user handbook explains how to utilize these accessories.

For model-specific instructions and advice, always refer to the user manual that comes with your Insta360 camera. Following these steps should assist you with unboxing, setting up, and utilizing your Insta360 camera to capture immersive material.

# CHAPTER TWO

# INSTA 360 X3 CAMERA FEATURES AND CONTROLS

Understanding your Insta360 camera's functions and controls is critical for maximizing its capabilities. While specifics vary between versions, the following are typical features and controls:

**Common Characteristics:**

360-Degree Capture: Insta360 cameras are ideal for creating immersive multimedia. They capture a full 360-degree perspective of the scene, enabling interactive exploration in both photos and films.

Stabilization: Many Insta360 cameras come with built-in stabilization technology that ensures smooth and steady filming even in dynamic or unsteady settings.

Live Streaming: Some models feature live streaming, which allows you to broadcast 360-degree content in real-time on sites like Facebook, YouTube, and other compatible services.

Multi-Lens System: Insta360 cameras frequently have many lenses or sensors, each of which captures a different aspect of the world. These pictures are stitched together to form a 360-degree panorama.

App operation: Use the Insta360 app to remotely operate your camera, alter settings, and preview or transfer content. The app serves as a single point for managing your camera's functionality.

Editing tools: Insta360 offers editing tools to help you improve and personalize your 360-degree photographs and videos. Examine the editing tools to see how you may apply effects, trim film, and more.

**Controls in Common:**

Power Button: This button, located on the camera's body, turns the camera on and off. To increase or decrease power, press and hold.

Use the shutter/record button to take images or to start/stop video recording. It's frequently located on the camera or accessible via the app.

Mode Button: If your camera has numerous shooting modes (photo, video, time-lapse, etc.), you can cycle through them by pressing the mode button.

Wi-Fi/Bluetooth Button: Use this button to enable Wi-Fi or Bluetooth connectivity to associate your camera with the Insta360 app. This button could also help with other wireless operations.

LEDs on the camera indicate the camera's status, such as power, Wi-Fi connection, or recording. Learn about the various light patterns and their meanings.

MicroSD Card Slot: For storage, insert a MicroSD card into the appropriate slot. Check if it has enough capacity and is compatible with your camera.

Charging Port: To recharge the camera's battery, connect the included charging cable to the charging port.

Settings Menu: Use physical buttons or the app to access the camera's settings. You can change the resolution, frame rate, exposure, and other parameters here.

Lens Protection: Some versions have lens caps or covers to keep the lenses safe when not in use.

Identify the placement of the microphones on the camera. Good audio is critical, especially when capturing videos.

User Manual: For extensive information on features, controls, and any special functionalities, always refer to the user manual relevant to your Insta360 camera model. It offers extensive instructions for using your camera efficiently and can be a useful resource for troubleshooting and getting the most out of your equipment.

# INTRODUCING THE INSTA360 APP AND DESKTOP SOFTWARE

To enhance the user experience and expand the creative possibilities of its 360-degree cameras, Insta360 offers a comprehensive ecosystem that includes both a mobile app and desktop software. Below is a detailed description of the Insta360 app and desktop applications:

**App Insta360:**

Compatibility with Platforms:

The Insta360 app is compatible with iOS and Android devices. It is available for download from the relevant app stores.

**Device Interconnection:**

The app acts as a connection point between your Insta360 camera and your mobile device. It enables remote control and content sharing by connecting to the camera via Wi-Fi or Bluetooth.

**Live Sneak Peek:**

The software allows users to see what the camera is collecting in real time. This tool is particularly helpful for framing photos and ensuring that the desired content is recorded.

**Control by remote:**

The app allows you to control your Insta360 camera from a distance. You can use your mobile device to change shooting modes, tweak settings, and capture photographs or movies.

**File Transfer and Administration:**

Using the software, you can easily transfer photographs and movies from your Insta360 camera to your mobile device. The software also includes features for organizing and managing your media assets.

**Editing Software:**

The Insta360 app features basic editing tools to help users improve their 360-degree photos and videos. Trimming, adding filters, and altering colors are examples of such functions.

**Viewing in 360 Degrees:**

Within the app, you may view and interact with your 360-degree content. Users can examine the whole scene taken by the camera by panning, tilting, and zooming.

**Sharing on Social Media:**

The app makes it simple to share material on prominent social networking platforms. Users can easily share their 360-degree photographs and films using the app.

**Desktop Insta360 Software:**

Compatibility with Platforms:

Insta360 offers desktop software that works with both Windows and macOS. The software can be downloaded and installed from the Insta360 website.

**Advanced Editing Options:**

When contrasted with the smartphone app, the desktop version has more powerful editing options. To generate finished 360-degree content, users can make detailed edits, add transitions, and apply special effects.

**Stitching:**

The desktop program features stitching capabilities for cameras with various lenses. It merges photos from each lens to generate a smooth and immersive 360-degree view.

**Options for Export:**

Users can export their altered content in a variety of formats and resolutions to suit various platforms and use cases. This offers professional video exports of excellent quality.

**Animation and keyframing:**

Users can use the desktop software to generate keyframes and animations to add dynamic movement to their 360-degree videos. This function improves the content's narrative skills.

**Advanced Options:**

To fine-tune the visual components of your 360-degree content, use advanced settings like exposure, white balance, and color grading.

**Third-Party Software Integration:**

Insta360's desktop software can be integrated with other editing software, increasing interoperability and allowing users to include 360-degree content in larger projects.

**User Interface and Help:**

Both the app and the desktop program have user-friendly interfaces, and Insta360 offers support and tutorials to assist customers in navigating the different functions and features. Users are advised to stay up to date with the newest versions of the app and software, since regular upgrades may introduce new features and enhancements.

## CHAPTER THREE

# CAPTURING 360-DEGREE PHOTOS

The technique of taking 360-degree photos with your Insta360 camera is simple. Here's a step-by-step tutorial to get you started:

**How to Use the Insta360 App:**

Turn on the camera:

Make sure your Insta360 camera is turned on and ready to take pictures.

Connect the Camera to the App: To connect to your camera, use the

Insta360 app on your smartphone or tablet. To connect to Wi-Fi or Bluetooth, follow the app's instructions.

Choose Photo Mode: In the app, select the photo mode. This mode is designed exclusively for taking 360-degree pictures.

Frame Your photo: Use the app's live preview to frame your photo. Remember that 360-degree photography captures everything around you, so consider the complete area.

Adjust Settings (Optional): Depending on the model of your camera, you may be able to change settings such as exposure, white balance, and ISO. Experiment with these parameters to get the photo quality you want.

Capture the Photo: Use the app's shutter button to take a 360-degree photo. Keep in mind the camera's stabilization and attempt to keep the camera steady for the best results.

Review and Edit (Optional): After taking the shot, you can go through it in the app and make changes. Some Insta360 cameras support basic editing via the app, such as applying filters or changing colors.

Save and Share: Save the photo to your device, and then share it immediately from the app to social media sites or other sharing channels if preferred.

Using the Camera Controls: If your Insta360 camera has physical controls, you can take images directly with the camera:

Turn on the camera: Switch on your Insta360 camera.

Select Photo Mode: To enter photo mode, press the mode button on the camera.

Frame Your Shot: To frame your shot, use the camera's viewfinder or any live preview screen.

Adjust Settings (Optional): If your camera supports manual settings, make any necessary adjustments.

Capture the snapshot: To capture the 360-degree snapshot, press the camera's shutter button.

Examine and Edit (Optional): If your camera has a screen, examine the collected image. Some cameras may provide basic editing functions right on the device.

Transfer to App (Optional): Transfer the shot from your camera to the Insta360 app for additional editing, sharing, or storage.

Remember to consult the user manual for your specific Insta360 camera model for complete instructions, since features and controls may differ between models. Experimenting with your camera and learning about its possibilities can help you gain confidence in shooting outstanding 360-degree photos.

## IMMERSIVE 360-DEGREE VIDEO SHOOTING

Shooting immersive 360-degree films with your Insta360 camera entails several processes that must be followed to ensure a smooth and engaging experience for your viewers. Here's a step-by-step approach to creating immersive 360-degree videos:

## *USING THE APP*

**Turn on the camera:**

Check that your Insta360 camera is turned on and has enough battery power.

Connect the Camera to the App by doing the following:

Connect to your camera via Wi-Fi or Bluetooth using the Insta360 app on your smartphone or tablet.

Choose Video Mode: In the app, select the video mode developed exclusively for 360-degree video recording.

Frame Your photo: Use the app's live preview to frame your photo. Take into account the complete 360-degree environment and make sure the camera is capturing the scenes you desire.

Adjust Settings (Optional): Depending on the model of your camera, you may be able to change settings such as resolution, frame rate, exposure, and white balance. Adapt these settings to your recording environment.

Begin recording:

To begin recording the 360-degree video, use the app's record button. To get smoother footage, keep the camera steady while recording.

Experiment with Camera Movement: To add dynamic features to your 360-degree film, experiment with different camera movements such as panning, tilting, or rotating. Experimenting with motion can improve the viewing experience.

Keep an eye on the camera's battery life, especially during extended recording sessions. If necessary, keep spare batteries on hand.

Stop Recording: When you've caught the necessary footage, press the app's stop button to cease the recording.

Review and Edit (Optional): After recording, go over the video on the app. Some Insta360 cameras support basic editing, such as trimming and effects.

**Save and distribute:**

Save the 360-degree movie to your device and share it via social media or other sharing channels right from the app.

***Using the Camera Controls: If your Insta360 camera has physical controls on the device, you can use the camera to record movies directly***:

Turn on the camera:

Start your Insta360 camera.

Select Video Mode: To enter video mode, press the mode button on the camera.

Compose Your Shot:

To frame your photo, use the camera's viewfinder or any live preview screen.

(Optional): If your camera has manual settings, modify them based on your recording environment.

Start Recording: To begin recording the 360-degree video, press the record button on the camera.

Play around with it. Camera Motion:

To add dynamic aspects to your video, move the camera in different directions.

Stop Recording: To end the recording, press the stop button on the camera.

Transfer to App (Optional): Transfer the video from your camera to the Insta360 app for additional editing, sharing, or storage.

Refer to the user manual for your specific Insta360 camera model for comprehensive instructions, as features and controls may differ between models. Practicing and experimenting with various filming approaches can assist you in mastering the skill of shooting immersive 360-degree videos.

## INSTA360 TIME-LAPSE AND HYPER-LAPSE

Using your Insta360 camera to create time-lapse and hyper-lapse films can add a dynamic aspect to your material. Here's a tutorial on how to record these types of videos:

**Time-Lapse:**

Turn on the camera:

Check that your Insta360 camera is turned on and has enough battery power.

Connect the Camera to the App by doing the following:

Connect to your camera via Wi-Fi or Bluetooth using the Insta360 app on your smartphone or tablet.

Choose Time-Lapse Mode: In the app, select the time-lapse mode. This mode is intended for recording photographs at predetermined intervals to generate a time-lapse effect.

Adjust Settings: Depending on the manufacturer of your camera, you may be able to set the interval between shots, the overall duration of the time-lapse, and other choices. Make changes based on your creative concept.

Compose Your Shot:

To frame your photo, use the app's live preview. Because the time-lapse will capture the changes over time, consider the full 360-degree environment.

Start Shooting: To begin the time-lapse recording, press the capture button. The camera will capture images at the intervals you specify.

Stop Shooting: When you've captured enough frames for your time-lapse, press the stop button.

Review and Edit (Optional): After recording, go into the app and review the time-lapse. Some Insta360 cameras provide basic editing, such as trimming and changing the playback speed.

Save and Share: Save the time-lapse to your device and share it immediately from the app on social networking sites or other ways.

A hyper-lapse is created by moving the camera between frames to give motion to the time-lapse. Here's how to make a hyper-lapse:

Steps 1-6 from the Time-Lapse Section should be followed:

As previously mentioned, set up your camera for time-lapse recording.

Plan Your Movement: Consider the path you want to take for the hyper-lapse. To get a smooth and visually appealing appearance, plan your moves carefully.

Begin Shooting: Begin capturing the time-lapse while carefully moving the camera along your planned path. The hyper-lapse effect will be produced by this movement.

Stop Shooting: When you've captured enough frames for your hyper-lapse, use the stop button.

**Optional review and editing:**

Review the hyper-lapse within the app after recording. Some Insta360 cameras provide basic editing, such as trimming and changing the playback speed.

Save and Share: Save the hyperlapse to your device and share it via social networking sites or other sharing channels right from the app.

Experimenting with varied intervals, movements, and environments can assist you in creating one-of-a-kind and engaging time-lapse and hyper-lapse videos. Always refer to the user manual for your specific Insta360 camera type for complete instructions and device settings.

# CHAPTER FOUR

# SHOOTING WITH LONG EXPOSURE AND LOW LIGHT

Using your Insta360 camera to capture long exposure and low-light images can yield beautiful and one-of-a-kind results. Here's a step-by-step approach to achieving these effects:

**Long-term exposure:**

Connect the Camera to the App by doing the following:

Connect to your camera via Wi-Fi or Bluetooth using the Insta360 app on your smartphone or tablet.

**Choose a Photo Mode:**

In the app, select the photo mode.

Change the settings:

Look for options related to exposure time or shutter speed, depending on your camera model. Set a longer exposure time to capture more light over time.

Adjust the camera's stability:

Long-exposure photographs are susceptible to movement. To avoid blurring caused by hand motions, use a tripod or position your camera on a firm surface.

**Compose Your Shot:**

Take into account the composition and lighting of your scene. Long-exposure photography is ideal for capturing light trails, star trails, and smooth water surfaces.

**Capture the Image:**

To begin the long exposure shot, press the capture button. Maintain camera stability throughout the exposure.

**Review and Modify (Optional):**

Examine the long exposure shot after it has been captured. Adjust the parameters or retake the image if necessary to attain the desired result.

**Save and distribute:**

Save the long exposure shot to your device and share it via social media or other sharing channels right from the app.

**Shooting in Low Light:**

Connect the Camera to the App by doing the following:

Connect to your camera via Wi-Fi or Bluetooth using the Insta360 app on your smartphone or tablet.

**Choose between Photo and Video Mode:**

In the app, select either photo or video mode depending on whether you want to capture a still photograph or video in low light.

**Change the ISO and exposure:**

Investigate your camera's ISO and exposure settings. Increase the ISO to improve light sensitivity in low-light situations. To balance brightness, adjust the exposure settings.

**Adjust the camera's stability:**

To avoid blurriness in low light, steadiness is essential. Place your camera on a tripod or a solid surface.

**Compose Your Shot:**

Consider the composition and pay special attention to items that stand out in poor light. Experiment with different perspectives and angles.

**Capture the Information:**

To begin capturing your low-light photo or video, press the capture button. Maintain the camera's stability throughout the process.

**Review and Modify (Optional):**

Examine the low-light content once it has been captured. If

necessary, adjust the parameters and consider experimenting with alternative ways to improve the outcome.

**Save and distribute:**

Save the low-light snapshot or video to your device and share it via social networking sites or other sharing channels directly from the app.

Experimenting with different settings, compositions, and shooting approaches with your Insta360 camera can help you master long-exposure and low-light photography. Always refer to the user manual for your specific camera model for complete instructions and device settings.

## A SUMMARY OF THE INSTA360 EDITING WORKFLOW

The Insta360 editing workflow entails using the Insta360 mobile app and, if necessary, the Insta360 Studio desktop software for more advanced editing. The following is a general editing workflow overview:

**Workflow for Editing an Insta360 App:**

1. Use the Insta360 app on your smartphone or tablet to connect the camera to the app.

Wi-Fi or Bluetooth your Insta360 camera to the app.

2. Import Media: Once connected, you may use the app to import photographs and videos from your camera.

3. Review and Trim: Within the app, review your captured content.

Trim or clip video segments, and make simple adjustments to your photos.

4. Use Filters and Effects: Experiment with different filters and effects to improve the appearance of your 360-degree photos and movies.

5. Change Settings: Some Insta360 cameras let you change settings like exposure, contrast, and saturation within the app.

6. Add Music (For Videos): If you're dealing with videos, you can

enhance the viewing experience by adding background music.

7. Export and share your edited content: Save your edited content to your smartphone.

From the app, share straight to social media networks or other sharing methods.

**Workflow for the Insta360 Studio Desktop Software:**

1. Import material: Copy the material from your Insta360 camera to your PC.

On your computer, launch Insta360 Studio.

2. Stitching (For Multi-Lens Cameras): If you have many lenses on your camera, Insta360 Studio can stitch the photos or videos together to produce a smooth 360-degree vision.

3. extensive Editing: When compared to the smartphone app, Insta360 Studio offers more extensive editing tools.

Make adjustments to the exposure, white balance, and color grading.

Use transitions, text, and keyframes to create dynamic effects.

4. Export options: Select export options such as resolution and file format based on your planned purpose.

5. Export the Final Edit: Save your changed content to your computer's desired location.

6. Share or Edit Further: Share the changed material directly from your computer, or use the exported file in another editing program to make additional changes.

**Tips:**

Always use the most recent version of the Insta360 app and Studio program to gain access to the most recent features and upgrades.

Experiment with various editing choices to find the style that works best for your content.

For further information on editing features and settings, go to the user manuals for your specific Insta360 camera model.

Remember that the precise features and capabilities of each Insta360 camera model may differ, so always consult the user manual for your specific device for the most up-to-date information.

## PHOTO EDITING WITH THE INSTA360 APP

Editing photos with the Insta360 app is a straightforward process that lets you enhance and customize your 360-degree images. Follow these steps to edit your photos using the Insta360 app:

**Link the Camera with the App:**

Launch the Insta360 app on your smartphone or tablet.

Connect your Insta360 camera to the app via Wi-Fi or Bluetooth.

**Import Your 360-Degree Photo:**

Once connected, view and import 360-degree photos from your camera to the app.

**Select the Photo for Editing:**

Choose the photo you wish to edit from the app's gallery.

**Basic Editing Capabilities:**

Use basic editing tools such as cropping, rotating, and straightening to fine-tune the composition of your photo.

**Experiment with Filters and Effects:**

Apply different filters and effects to add a creative touch to your photo. The app offers a variety of preset filters to choose from.

**Fine-Tune Exposure and Color:**

Adjust exposure, contrast, saturation, and other color parameters to enhance the overall appearance of your photo.

**Delete or Add Objects (Optional):**

Some Insta360 cameras and the app allow you to delete or add objects to your photos. Explore these features for additional editing options.

**Save Your Edits:**

Once you're satisfied with your adjustments, save the edited photo.

**Export or Share the Edited Photo:**

Save the edited photo to your device or share it directly from the app to social media platforms or other sharing channels.

**Advanced Editing (Insta360 Studio - Optional):**

For more advanced editing options, transfer your photos to the Insta360 Studio desktop software. This software offers features such as stitching, keyframing, and more detailed adjustments.

By following these steps, you can effectively edit and enhance your 360-degree photos using the Insta360 app, making your images stand out and ready for sharing.

**Tips:**

Filters: Experiment with different filters to discover how they affect the atmosphere and style of your shot.

Adjust Lighting: Pay close attention to exposure settings to create a well-lit photograph.

Utilize Advanced Options Wisely: Object removal and insertion may not be appropriate for every shot, so use them sparingly.

For extensive instructions on the editing features accessible in the app, always refer to the user manual for your Insta360 camera model. The program is intended to be user-friendly, so feel free to explore and experiment with your

360-degree photos to reach the desired effects.

## VIDEO EDITING WITH THE INSTA360 STUDIO

Using Insta360 Studio to edit films allows you to enhance and modify your 360-degree video material with more complex tools. Here's a step-by-step tutorial for editing videos with Insta360 Studio:

1. Import Your 360° Video:

Transfer your Insta360 camera's 360-degree footage to your PC.

On your computer, launch Insta360 Studio.

2. Preview Your Video: After importing the video, you may see it on the Insta360 Studio interface.

3. Stitching (For Multi-Lens Cameras): If you have numerous lenses on your camera, Insta360 Studio can stitch the images or videos together to produce a smooth 360-degree vision. Some models may not require this step.

4. Trimming the Video: Trim the video to remove any unneeded

areas. Adjust the in and out points to keep only the portion you desire.

5. extensive Editing: When compared to the smartphone app, Insta360 Studio offers more extensive editing features.

To improve the visual quality of your movie, adjust the exposure, white balance, and color grading.

Add keyframes to control the orientation and movement of the camera during playback.

Incorporate transitions between scenes for a more seamless viewing experience.

6. Include Text and Annotations: Include text, annotations, or titles within the video to add context or information.

7. Add Music (Optional): You can import and synchronize audio tracks if your video lacks audio or if you wish to add background music.

8. Export Options: Select export options such as resolution and file format based on your intended

purpose. Insta360 Studio offers a variety of export choices for various platforms.

9. Export the Final Edit: Once you've finished editing, save the video to your computer's desired location.

10. Share or Edit Further: Share the changed material directly from your computer, or use the exported file in other editing tools to make additional changes.

Tips:

Play around with keyframes: Keyframes allow you to control the direction and movement of the camera over time. For dynamic effects, try out different keyframe settings.

Smooth transitions between scenes help to create a more polished and professional-looking video.

Examine Your Changes: Before exporting, evaluate your modified video to confirm that it satisfies your creative vision.

For extensive instructions on the editing options available in Insta360 Studio, always refer to the user manual for your specific Insta360 camera model. The software is intended to give a powerful set of editing capabilities for 360-degree videos, allowing you to produce immersive and entertaining material.

# CHAPTER FIVE

# VIRTUAL TOUR CREATION INTRODUCTION

Creating a virtual tour entails capturing and displaying a series of photographs or videos that allow viewers to remotely explore an area. It's an effective approach to exhibit spaces while also providing an immersive experience. Here's a primer on creating virtual tours:

1. Preparation:

Define Your Goal:

Define the aim of your virtual tour clearly. Are you promoting a piece of real estate, an educational institution, or a business? Knowing what you want to achieve will direct your strategy.

Select a Location:

Determine the space or location you want to photograph. Prepare the path that spectators will take during the virtual tour.

2. Camera: Select a camera that is capable of 360-degree capture. Many 360-degree cameras, such as

the Insta360 or Ricoh Theta, are specifically built for this purpose. You can also use a smartphone with a suitable app.

Tripod: Stability is essential for a smooth virtual tour. To keep the camera stable throughout capture, use a tripod.

3. 360-Degree Content Capture:

Positioning: To get a thorough view, place the camera in the center of the space. Make sure it's at the right height for the greatest view.

Capture Images or movies: Use your camera to take a series of images or movies at various spots around the region. Take note of lighting and uniformity between shots.

4. After-Processing:

If your camera records many lenses, utilize stitching software (typically provided by the camera maker) to combine the photos into a continuous 360-degree view.

Editing: Depending on your camera, you may have editing

capabilities. To improve the visual quality, change the exposure, color, and other settings.

5. Select a Virtual Tour Platform: Select a virtual tour platform to host and display your content. Matterport, Kuula, and even social networking networks that enable 360-degree multimedia are popular possibilities.

Upload and Arrange: Upload your 360-degree photographs or movies to the platform of your choice. Arrange them to guide viewers through the tour in the desired order.

6. Participation:

Add Points of Interest (POIs): Some virtual tour platforms allow you to add POIs with additional information, photographs, or links. By combining these features, you may increase the engagement of your tour.

Ensure that visitors can easily move around the tour. For orientation, include directional arrows or a map.

7. Collaboration:

Once your virtual tour is complete, distribute the links on your website, social media, and other channels. For convenient access, consider embedding the tour directly on your website.

8. Encourage Interaction: Encourage visitors to interact with the virtual tour. Consider including call-to-action elements like contact forms or links to related information.

Collect Feedback:

Gather input from spectators to improve future virtual tours. Analyze the hosting platform's engagement stats.

Creating a virtual tour necessitates careful preparation, the capture of high-quality content, and the use of interactive features to captivate viewers. As technology progresses, so do the capabilities for making virtual tours, opening up new avenues for immersive storytelling.

# STITCHING AND CONNECTING MANY 360-DEGREE PHOTOS

Creating a cohesive panoramic view for virtual tours or immersive experiences requires stitching and integrating many 360-degree photos. A general approach to stitching and connecting various 360-degree pictures is available here:

1. Select Stitching Software:

Use the stitching software offered by your 360-degree camera's manufacturer. Many cameras, such as the Insta360 and Ricoh Theta, include stitching software. You can also utilize third-party applications such as Adobe Photoshop or PTGui.

2. Upload Photos to Computer: Upload the 360-degree photos from your camera to your computer. Assemble all of the photographs you want to stitch into a single folder for convenient access.

3. Launch Stitching Software: Start your computer's stitching software.

4. Import photographs: Open the stitching software and import the 360-degree photographs. To load the photos, follow the software's instructions.

5. The stitching process will evaluate the photographs and automatically align and blend them to create a seamless panorama. Depending on the software and the number of photographs, this process may take some time.

6. Adjust Settings (Optional): Some stitching software lets you change settings including stitching process,

alignment, and output format. Experiment with these settings to get the desired outcome.

7. Preview the Stitched Panorama: Once the stitching process is complete, open the software and preview the stitched panorama. Make sure there aren't any noticeable seams or distortions.

8. Export the Stitched Panorama: Save or export the stitched panorama in the format that best suits your needs. JPEG and PNG are two popular formats.

9. Repeat for Additional Panoramas: If you need to assemble more 360-degree photographs, repeat the technique for each set of images.

10. Connecting many Panoramas: To connect and display many panoramas, use a virtual tour or 360-degree video development platform. You can generate a series of linked panoramas using platforms such as Kuula, Matterport, or even custom online solutions.

**Tips:**

Overlap: During the capture process, ensure that there is enough overlap between neighboring photographs. This allows the stitching software to precisely align the photos.

Keep Consistent Exposure: To avoid apparent differences in lighting, keep the exposure settings identical throughout all images.

Use a Tripod: To keep the camera stable when taking images, use a tripod. This reduces the possibility of stitching problems caused by camera movement.

Check for Stitching mistakes: Carefully examine the stitched panoramas for stitching mistakes such as apparent seams or distortions. If necessary, adjust the parameters or re-stitch.

Creating a smooth link between several 360-degree shots requires a combination of high-quality image capture, the use of proper stitching software, and the selection of an acceptable platform for displaying the connected panoramas. For further instructions, always refer to the user manual for your specific camera and stitching software.

# IMPLEMENTING INTERACTIVE ELEMENTS IN VIRTUAL TOURS

Including interactive components in virtual tours increases user engagement and creates a more immersive experience. Here are some examples of common interactive elements you can include in your virtual tours:

## 1. Hotspots:

Hotspots are clickable sections of the virtual tour that bring up additional content or information.

Case Studies:

Give specifics about certain things or features.

External websites or resources should be linked to.

Include hotspot-related videos or photographs.

## 2. POIs (Points of Interest):

Points of Interest are distinct areas inside the virtual tour that provide further context or information.

Case Studies:

Highlight key features or landmarks.

Give historical or educational background information.

Include any relevant photographs, videos, or audio clips.

### 3. interactive Maps:

Include a map that allows customers to travel between different areas of the virtual tour.

Case Studies:

Improve navigation by providing a high-level summary of the entire tour.

Allow consumers to navigate directly to certain areas of interest.

4. Personalized Navigation Paths:

Create specified paths or tours that take users through the virtual space in a specific order.

Case Studies:

Tell a tale by directing users in chronological order.

Highlight important areas or characteristics in a specific sequence.

## 5. Videos in 360 Degrees:

Definition: Incorporate 360-degree videos into the virtual tour to offer a layer of engagement.

Case Studies:

Display exciting scenes or activities.

When opposed to static visuals, they provide a more immersive experience.

## 6. Forms or surveys embedded:

Include forms or surveys into the virtual tour to capture user feedback or data.

Case Studies:

Collect user feedback or preferences.

Gather leads and contact information.

## 7. Personalized Audio Narration:

Definition: To provide more information, add audio narration at select points in the virtual tour.

Case Studies:

Use voice-guided narration to improve your storytelling.

Explain details that may not be obvious from the visuals alone.

Integrating Social Media:

Incorporate social network sharing buttons or feeds into the virtual tour.

Case Studies:

Allow users to share their virtual tour experience via social media.

Include social media feeds on the place or issue.

**9. Web Content Embedded:**

External web information, such as web pages or articles, should be embedded into the virtual tour.

Case Studies:

Provide extra information gleaned from outside sources.

Provide a link to related articles or resources.

**Elements of Gamification:**

Incorporate gamification components like quizzes, challenges, or incentives into the virtual tour.

Case Studies:

Increase the interactivity and enjoyment of the encounter.

Encourage exploration and participation.

**Tips:**

Maintain User-Friendliness: Make sure that interactive features are straightforward to utilize.

Check for mobile compatibility by ensuring that your interactive features perform properly on both desktop and mobile devices.

Design Balance: Avoid cluttering the virtual tour with too many interactive components. To avoid a cluttered user experience, strike a balance.

Thoroughly test: Thoroughly test the virtual tour to find any problems with interactive features and to ensure a smooth user experience.

Including these interactive components in your virtual tours can considerably improve their overall quality and engagement level. Choose aspects that correspond to your objectives and the type of experience you want to deliver to your audience.

## CONTENT UPLOADING TO SOCIAL MEDIA PLATFORMS

Uploading 360-degree content to social media platforms, such as images or videos, allows you to share immersive experiences with your audience. Because different sites support 360-degree material differently, here's a general strategy for uploading to some prominent social media networks:

**1. 360 Photos on Facebook:**

Access your Facebook profile or page.

Select "Photo/Video" from the top of the news feed.

Choose the 360-degree photo you want to upload.

Choose your audience settings, tag individuals, and add a caption.

Select "Post."

360 Videos: Repeat the process, but this time select the video file.

Check that your video is properly prepared for 360 playback.

Choose your audience settings, tag individuals, and add a caption.

Select "Post."

## 2. YouTube 360 Videos: Login to your YouTube account.

At the top, select the video camera icon.

Choose "Upload video."

Select the 360-degree video file.

Fill in the blanks with a title, description, and tags.

Check the box next to "This video is 360" under "Advanced settings."

Click "Publish" or "Private" if you want to go over it first.

## 3. Instagram: 360 Photos: Launch the Instagram application.

To make a new post, press the "+" button.

Choose the 360-degree photo from your camera roll.

Adjust the filters and captions as needed.

Select "Share."

360 Videos: Repeat the previous steps, but this time select the 360 video file.

Check that the video is properly formatted.

Captions should be edited and added.

Select "Share."

**4. Twitter: 360 Photos: Write a new tweet.**

Select the 360 photo by clicking the photo icon.

Text and hashtags can be added.

Tap "Tweet."

360 Videos: Repeat the previous steps, but this time select the 360 video file.

Check that your video is properly formatted.

Text and hashtags can be added.

Tap "Tweet."

5. LinkedIn 360 Photos: Make a new post on your LinkedIn profile or company page using 360 photos.

Select your 360 photos by clicking on the image icon.

Enter a post description and press "Post."

360 Videos: Repeat the previous steps, but this time select the 360 video file.

Check that the video is properly formatted.

Enter a post description and press "Post."

**Tips:**

Formatting: Make certain that your 360-degree footage is properly prepared for each platform. Some platforms may require particular information to detect 360 content.

Encourage engagement on your 360-degree posts by asking questions, providing captions, and replying to comments.

Platform-Specific Characteristics: Investigate 360-degree multimedia platform-specific features, such as Instagram's interactive aspects or YouTube's spatial audio.

Remember to examine each social media platform's unique restrictions and needs for 360-

degree content, since their features and capabilities may change over time.

## CHAPTER SIX

# CREATING AND SHARING 360-DEGREE PHOTOSPHERES ON GOOGLE MAPS

You may add immersive material to Google Maps by creating and uploading 360-degree photospheres. Here's a step-by-step tutorial for making and sharing 360-degree photospheres with the Google Street View app:

**How to Make 360-Degree Photospheres:**

Install the Google Street View app:

Check that your mobile device has the Google Street View app loaded. You may get it from the App Store for iOS or the Google Play Store for Android.

**Launch the app:**

On your device, open the Google Street View app.

**Making a New Photosphere:**

To make a new photosphere, tap the camera symbol in the bottom-right area.

Follow the on-screen instructions: The app will walk you through the steps. Begin by pointing the camera toward the orange dots, and the app will capture photographs as you go.

**Capture the Complete Sphere:**

Move the camera in all directions until you've completed a full circle to ensure you catch the entire sphere.

**Examine and retake (if necessary):**

Examine the photosphere you captured. If any part is missing or you are dissatisfied, you can retake the test.

Give Your Photosphere a Name:

Give your photosphere a name and any further information you want to include.

Publish to Google Maps: Once your photosphere is complete, you may opt to publish it to Google Maps.

Google Maps 360-Degree Photosphere Sharing:

**Launch the Google Maps app:**

On your mobile device, open the Google Maps app.

Find the Location:

Determine where you want to place your 360-degree photosphere.

View Photos:

To open the location, tap on it, and then on the photo icon.

Add a Photo: To add a photo, tap the "+" icon.

**Choose Your Photosphere:**

Select the 360-degree photosphere from your gallery.

**Include specifics:**

Add any more information to your photosphere, such as a description or a title.

**Publish to Google Maps:**

To post your 360-degree photosphere to Google Maps, press the "Post" button.

Verify the Upload: Your photosphere will be checked for accuracy. It will be visible on Google Maps once approved.

**Tips:**

Quality is Important: To boost the overall quality, make sure your photosphere is well-captured with decent lighting and minimum movement.

Investigate Contributions: Check the "Contributions" area of the Google Maps app to check how many views your submitted photospheres have received.

post on Social Media: To improve visibility, post the URL to your

Google Maps photosphere on social media or with friends.

By generating and uploading 360-degree photospheres on Google Maps, you add to the platform's rich visual content while also providing users with immersive experiences of various locales.

## COMMON ISSUE WITH INSTA360 AND SOLUTIONS

Insta360 cameras, like any other technology, can have problems from time to time. Here are some typical Insta360 camera difficulties and potential solutions:

1. connectivity issues: Difficulty attaching the Insta360 camera to the app or computer.

Solution: Turn on Bluetooth and Wi-Fi on your device.

Restart the camera as well as the app.

Allow your phone to forget the device and reconnect.

Upgrade the Insta360 app to the most recent version.

2. Stitching Errors: Issues with stitching in the final 360-degree photo or video.

Solution: Make certain that the camera lenses are clean.

Upgrade the camera's firmware to the most recent version.

Use memory cards and formats that are recommended.

Check for stitching software updates.

3. Battery Life Issues: Issue: Inadequate battery life or the camera shutting down suddenly.

Solution: Charge the camera completely before using it.

Make sure to use the original charging cable and adaptor.

Examine for firmware updates that may address battery problems.

4. Overheating: Issue: The camera grows abnormally heated while in use.

Solution: Make sure the camera is properly ventilated.

Avoid using the camera in direct sunlight for long periods.

Reduce the resolution or frame rate of the camera.

5. Insta360 App Crashes or Freezes: Issue: The Insta360 app crashes or freezes.

Close and reopen the app as a workaround.

Remove the app cache.

Upgrade the app to the most recent version.

Check for compatibility with the operating system of your device.

6. Playback Issues: Some devices have difficulty playing back 360-degree videos.

Solution: Use a device or player that supports 360-degree video playback.

Ensure that the video file is properly formatted for the selected playback device.

7. Blurriness or Focusing Issues: The photo or video appears hazy or out of focus.

Solution: Use a microfiber cloth to clean the camera lenses.

Examine the lenses for a protective film.

For clear photos, ensure suitable lighting conditions.

8. GPS Not Working: The GPS data is not being recorded appropriately.

Solution: Make sure the camera has a clear view of the sky to receive GPS signals.

Update the firmware and app on the camera to the most recent releases.

Examine the app's GPS settings.

9. Problems with App linking: Difficulty linking the camera with the app.

Solution: Remove the gadget from your phone and reconnect.

Restart the camera as well as the app.

Check that your device's Bluetooth and Wi-Fi are both turned on.

Markdown for Audio Quality Issues

-Problem: Videos with poor audio quality or no sound.

- Workaround:

- Make sure the microphone on the camera is not obscured.

- Update the firmware of the camera.

- Check the app's audio settings.

For detailed troubleshooting methods for your camera model, always consult the official Insta360 website or user manual. If problems persist, contact Insta360's customer service for assistance.

## TIPS FOR EXTENDING THE LIFE OF YOUR BATTERY AND STORAGE

Getting the most out of your Insta360 camera requires optimizing battery life and storage. Here are some pointers to help you extend battery life and effectively manage storage:

**Increasing Battery Life:**

Charge completely before use:

To ensure optimal battery life, fully charge your Insta360 camera before use.

Make use of the original charger:

To charge your camera, use the included charging wire and adaptor. Using third-party chargers may result in subpar performance.

**Firmware Upgrade:**

Keep the firmware on your camera up to date. Manufacturers frequently offer upgrades that improve power management.

Control Wi-Fi and Bluetooth:

To save battery life, turn off Wi-Fi and Bluetooth when not in use. Use these features only when you require remote control or communication.

**Capture Settings Should Be Optimized:**

If high-quality film isn't required for your unique use case, reduce the resolution or frame rate. This has the potential to greatly increase battery life.

If available, use Power Save Mode:

Some cameras provide a power-saving mode that reduces performance while increasing battery life. When recording or capturing is less difficult, choose this mode.

**Avoid High Temperatures:**

Operating your camera in extremely hot or cold temperatures can influence battery performance. Maintain the camera's temperature within the recommended range.

**Disable Auto Shutdown:**

Consider disabling your camera's auto-shutdown feature during

longer shoots to avoid interruptions.

**Spare batteries should be carried:**

Carry spare batteries if feasible, especially for long photography sessions.

When not in use, turn off the power:

To save battery life, turn off the camera while you're not actively using it.

**Storage Administration:**

Invest in High-Capacity Memory Cards:

To accommodate more footage, invest in high-capacity, high-speed memory cards.

**Format cards regularly:**

Format your memory cards in the camera regularly. This contributes to optimal performance and prevents file corruption.

**Unwanted Content Should Be Removed:**

To free up space, delete useless photos and movies regularly. To avoid unintentional deletions, do this when your camera is not linked to the app.

**Promptly transfer files:**

To free up space on the camera, immediately transfer your content to a computer or external storage device.

**Change the Capture Settings:**

Based on your requirements, select the appropriate resolution and bitrate parameters. Higher settings require more storage space.

**If compression is available, use it:**

Some cameras have compression features that allow you to reduce file sizes without sacrificing quality significantly.

**Upload to the Cloud:**

Consider automatically uploading content to cloud storage if your camera enables it to keep your camera's storage free.

**Storage Capacity of the Monitor:**

Check your camera's available storage capacity frequently to avoid running out of space on critical occasions.

**Keep spare memory cards on hand:**

Carry spare memory cards in case one of your cameras' memory cards runs out.

By following these guidelines, you can ensure that your Insta360 camera has enough battery life and storage space for your creative pursuits. Specific rules and recommendations should always be found in your camera's user manual.

## STAYING CURRENT WITH NEW FEATURES AND FIRMWARE UPDATES

Updating the firmware on your Insta360 camera is critical for accessing new features, enhancing performance, and resolving potential difficulties. Here are the processes for updating the firmware, as well as some pointers for remaining up to speed on new features:

**Firmware Update:**

Examine for Updates:

Check for firmware upgrades regularly using the official Insta360 website or the Insta360 app. Manufacturers frequently provide updates to improve camera performance and include new features.

Firmware can be downloaded here:

If a firmware update is available, download it from the official website or follow the in-app prompts to download it directly to your camera.

**Firmware Transfer to Camera:**

Using a card reader or by connecting the camera to your computer, copy the downloaded firmware file to the root directory of your camera's microSD card.

**Download and install the update:**

Put the microSD card containing the firmware file into your camera.

When you turn on the camera, it should automatically detect the firmware update. To install the update, follow the on-screen instructions.

**Wait for the job to be finished:**

Allow the updating procedure to finish. During the update, keep the camera switched on and connected to a reliable power source.

**Reboot the camera:**

When the update is complete, restart your camera to have the changes take effect.

**Keeping Up with New Features:**

Notifications Subscription:

Subscribe to Insta360 email notifications or newsletters to receive updates on new firmware releases and features.

Follow us on social media and in forums:

Connect with Insta360 on social media and online forums. Companies frequently promote new features and changes on social media sites such as Instagram, Twitter, and community forums.

Visit the App Store:

If your camera is linked to a mobile app, check the app store frequently for updates. App upgrades frequently include compatibility enhancements and new features.

Visit the Official Website: Check the official Insta360 website regularly for announcements, release notes, and firmware updates. The website's help or downloads section is a useful way to find the most recent firmware.

Participate in Beta Programs (if they exist):

Some manufacturers provide beta programs for users who want to test new features before they are released officially. Consider participating in these programs if they are accessible, but be mindful that beta versions may contain flaws.

Check out the Release Notes:

When a new firmware update is available, make sure to read the release notes. Manufacturers often give details about the updates' enhancements and new features.

Contact Customer Service:

If you have particular questions about firmware updates or encounter problems, contact customer service. They can offer advice and guarantee you're using the most recent firmware version.

By remaining watchful and constantly pursuing updates, you can ensure that your Insta360 camera has the most up-to-date features and upgrades, boosting your overall experience with the device. To avoid problems, always follow the manufacturer's instructions and guidelines when updating firmware.

## CHAPTER SEVEN

## UNBOXING OF THE INSTA 360 X3

The Insta360 X3 comes with a carrying case, a USB-C charging cable, and a small instruction manual. To use your Insta360 X3, you will need a microSD card. I recommend the SanDisk Extreme Pro, as it offers the fastest speeds. Keep in mind that 360° videos are quite large, so lower-capacity SD cards may fill up quickly.

To charge the X3, insert the USB cable into the charging port on the side of the camera. A full charge should take approximately 90 minutes.

The power button is located on the side of the camera. When you power on the camera, you will be prompted to activate it using the Insta360 app.

**ACCESSING THE APP**

Install the Insta360 app on your phone and enable both Bluetooth and Wi-Fi. Launch the app and select the "Link to Camera" option. Your phone will search for the camera and display it when found. The app will prompt you to confirm that you want to use the camera. Go to your camera and confirm that it is activated. The camera is now fully operational.

**Camera Controls and Design**

The Insta360 X3 is primarily an action camera. It's compact and light, with rubber grips. In addition to the power button, there is a quick menu button, a shutter button, and a media button.

Although HDR video mode allows you to improve the quality of your video without editing, manual settings are not available.

The photo modes follow a similar trend, with 360 photo mode allowing you to manually manage settings and HDR photos having higher quality but less manual options.

Overall, I recommend using HDR modes during the day but switching to manual mode at night or inside.

## SUGGESTIONS FOR ACCESSORIES

The invisible selfie stick is my number one recommended accessory. This is pretty much required for 90% of the images I take with the Insta360 X3.

There are a few options from Insta360 or other providers, but you need one to get the most out of this camera. You should also acquire a tiny tripod for still video.

There are numerous different accessories available, but they are optional depending on the type of video you intend to record.

**CAPTURING YOUR FIRST VIDEOS**

Take your camera outside where there is adequate lighting. The camera may also be used indoors and in low light, but this requires more advanced camera settings tuning that is beyond the scope of this beginner's approach. More advanced tutorials will be available soon if you subscribe.

Ensure that the highest resolution of 5.7K is selected. In good lighting, you can leave the rest of the settings on Automatic.

Attach your camera to your invisible selfie stick and extend it halfway or all the way. Place the selfie stick diagonally behind you to film third-person footage. Hold the stick in front of you for first-person shots.

Hold the stick straight up for 20 to 30 seconds if you are surrounded by fascinating features.

You can capture longer still films if you have a tripod. For about a minute, turn off the camera. To obtain a slightly different appearance, adjust the height of the tripod.

These are the basic 360 camera pictures that allow you to capture yourself as well as the area around you using the invisible selfie stick effect.

Of course, you could be moving when taking these photos. Because the X3 has outstanding stabilization, you can employ these techniques while walking, running, or riding a bike, scooter, or skates.

There are thousands of different shooting strategies for generating distinctive footage with your Insta360 X3, but starting with these more basic shots and experimenting from there is a fantastic place to start.

When in single lens mode, you use the camera as you would your phone or a GoPro. The major consideration is the field of vision, which goes from more natural Linear to widescreen activity.

## VIDEO EDITING FOR THE FIRST TIME

The editing step is where the majority of the creativity occurs when generating videos with the X3. Connect the Insta360 App to your X3. Navigate to the gallery to view your clips. Choose your first clip. You have two options for reframing: quick edit and manual.

Snap editing allows you to reframe your video by physically moving your phone. It's similar to using your phone as a camera to direct your shot.

Manually reframing allows you to select keyframes along your video that will pan from one point to another slowly. You can also zoom in and out in both of these modes. You have a lot more options in the manual reframing editor, such as altering the pace, trimming, and color correction.

**EXPORTING YOUR VIDEOS**

When you're finished editing, click the export option and choose reframed video. You should pick "custom" from the "quick export" menu. You can adjust the video quality settings here. Select the highest possible resolution and a bitrate of at least 60MBPS.

If you're an aspiring YouTuber or filmmaker, the Insta360 X3 is a fun device to own. This Insta360 product may help you add unique effects to your films, such as a clear 360° viewpoint, pseudo drone shots, and even a small planet. You can also add accessories to it and attach it to different surfaces. Along with all of this, did you know that the

Insta360 X3 can also be used as a webcam?

Yes, you read that correctly. A new firmware update for the Insta360 X3 has been released, allowing the camera to function as a webcam replacement. The X3's 360° view can provide a broader perspective to your meetings while ensuring high-quality video transmission.

## Introduction: Using the Insta360 X3 as a Webcam

The Insta360 X3 may function as a high-quality webcam for video conferencing, live streaming, and virtual meetings. This article will walk you through the process of configuring your Insta360 X3 as a webcam, assuring the highest possible video quality and experience.

**Setting up the Insta360 X3 as a webcam requires preparation.**

Charge your camera. Make sure your Insta360 X3 is fully charged or linked to an external power supply.

Install the latest firmware. Make sure your camera has the most recent firmware installed. Check for updates using the Insta360 app or website.

**Connect to Your Computer:**

Connect the Insta360 X3 to your computer via a USB connection. Make sure the connection is secure.

**Open the Insta360 Link Software:**

Download and install the Insta360 Link program from Insta360's official website. This program is required to enable webcam capability.

**Configuring the camera:**

To switch to webcam mode, turn on your Insta360 X3 and navigate to the settings menu. Choose the option to enter "Webcam Mode." This parameter can also be accessed via the Insta360 app.

**Select Camera Mode:**

Select the desired camera mode (such as 360° or conventional wide-angle). For most video conferencing applications, the normal wide-angle mode is suggested.

**Adjusting camera settings:**

Adjust the resolution and frame rate settings to your preferences. Higher resolutions and frame rates improve quality but may necessitate more bandwidth and processing power.

Configure your field of view (FOV) settings to guarantee optimal framing. The Insta360 Link software allows you to zoom in and out, as well as modify the field of view.

**Set up your video conferencing software:**

Select the Insta360 X3 as your webcam.

Navigate to the settings menu in your video conferencing program (such as Zoom, Microsoft Teams, or Google Meet).

Choose Insta360 X3 from the list of available webcams.

**Test the camera:**

Test the camera within the software to confirm that it is working properly. Adjust the camera's angle and lighting as appropriate.

Tips for Using the Insta360 X3 as a Webcam: Optimal Lighting

Make sure your face is well-lit, whether with natural or artificial lighting. Avoid backlighting, which can make your face appear darker.

**Camera placement:**

Position the Insta360 X3 at eye level for a natural and engaging view. To hold the camera steady, use a tripod or a firm surface.

**Audio Quality:**

Using an external microphone or headset will improve audio quality. The Insta360 X3's built-in microphone is functional; however, an additional microphone can produce crisper audio.

**Background:**

Choose a clean, professional background. Avoid clutter and distractions to maintain the audience's attention on you during the video chat.

**Stable Connection:**

Make sure your computer has a steady and fast internet connection to avoid lag or disconnections during your video conversation.

**Regular updates:**

Update your Insta360 X3 and Insta360 Link software to take advantage of the most recent features and upgrades.

**Troubleshooting: Common Issues**

Camera Not Recognized:

Make sure the USB cable is securely connected to the camera and the computer.

Restart the Insta360 X3 and your computer. If the problem persists, try switching to a different USB port or cable.

**Poor video quality:**

Check your lighting arrangement and change the resolution settings in the Insta360 Link program.

Make sure your internet connection is reliable and has enough bandwidth.

**Audio Issues:**

If the built-in microphone does not produce good audio quality, use an external microphone or headset.

Check the audio settings in your video conferencing software to confirm that the appropriate microphone is selected.

**Software crashes or freezes.**

Make sure your PC fulfills the system requirements for the Insta360 Link program.

Close superfluous applications to free up system resources, then restart the Insta360 Link software.

By following these instructions and best practices, you may use the Insta360 X3 as a webcam to improve the quality of your video chats and online meetings by providing immersive 360° video and higher image quality.

# LIVE STREAMING WITH THE INSTA360 X3

## Setting Up a Live Stream

Live streaming with the Insta360 X3 is an effective way to share immersive experiences in real-time with your target audience. Here is a step-by-step tutorial to help you get started:

**Preparation:**

Charge Your Camera: Make sure your Insta360 X3 is completely charged to prevent interruptions throughout your stream.

Stable Internet Connection: Ensure that your internet connection is stable and speedy. A Wi-Fi connection is suggested for optimal quality.

**Connecting the camera:**

Turn on the camera. Turn on your Insta360 X3.

Open the Insta360 app. Connect your camera to the Insta360 app on your smartphone via Bluetooth or Wi-Fi.

**Configuring live stream settings:**

To access live stream mode, open the Insta360 app and select the live stream option. This is normally located on the main menu or within the shooting modes.

**Select Platform:**

Choose your streaming platform (for example, YouTube, Facebook, or Twitch). The app will walk you through signing into your account and obtaining the appropriate permissions.

**Stream URL and key:**

To create custom RTMP streams, input the stream URL and key provided by your streaming platform. This is typically located inside the platform's live stream settings.

**Configure settings:**

Set your resolution, bitrate, and other options. Higher resolutions and bitrates improve quality but use more bandwidth.

**Start the Live Stream:**

Preview: Before going live, check your stream to ensure everything appears good. The Insta360 app often includes a preview capability.

Go Live: Once you're finished with the configuration, click the "Go Live" button. Your stream will begin streaming to your chosen platform.

**Monitor the Stream:**

Check the app: Use the Insta360 app to track your stream in real-time. If the platform allows you to see viewer comments and feedback, you can do so.

Adjusting Settings: During the stream, you can change some parameters, such as moving between viewpoints or adjusting the volume.

## **BEST PRACTICES FOR LIVESTREAMING**

To ensure a smooth and professional live streaming experience with the Insta360 X3, use these best practices:

**Preparation and Test:**

Test Your Setup: Perform a test stream before your live broadcast. This aids in detecting any potential issues with your system, such as connectivity or audio issues.

Plan your content. Outline what you want to cover during your livestream. A comprehensive plan will help keep your content engaging and organized.

**Optimize your environment.**

Lighting: Use good lighting to improve video quality. Natural light is best, but if you're indoors, add some lighting to enliven the atmosphere.

Background: Select a clean, distraction-free background. A crowded background can draw attention away from your main content.

**Audio Quality:**

Use External Microphones: If possible, use an external microphone to get crisper sounds.

Built-in microphones may detect unwanted sounds.

Check audio levels: Check your audio levels to ensure they aren't too loud (producing distortion) or too low (making it difficult to hear).

**Engage with your audience.**

Encourage viewers to ask questions and interact with you while streaming. Respond to comments and make your audience feel engaged.

Consistency is key: stream regularly to grow and sustain your audience. Consistency allows readers to know when to expect your information.

**Stabilization and Camera Movement:**

Use a Tripod or Stabilizer: To achieve stable and professional-looking footage, mount your Insta360 X3 on a tripod or with a stabilizer.

Smooth Movements: If you want to avoid unsettling your viewers, move the camera slowly and smoothly.

**Network and Data Management:**

Stable Connection: If possible, use a wired connection. If you use Wi-Fi, be sure it's dependable and fast enough for streaming.

Monitor Data Usage: Streaming consumes a lot of data. Keep an eye on your data usage, particularly if you have a limited data plan.

**Backup Plans:**

Prepare a backup plan in the event of technological difficulties. This could be a previously recorded video or a supplementary streaming device.

By following these steps and best practices, you can produce high-quality, entertaining live streams with your Insta360 X3, assuring a great experience for both you and your viewers.

**THE END**

www.ingramcontent.com/pod-product-compliance
Lightning Source LLC
Chambersburg PA
CBHW050210230526
45470CB00001B/315